Mansions of the Heart

STUDY GUIDE
for Personal & Group Reflection

R. Thomas Ashbrook

and

Ted Wueste

Published by Mansions Study Guide Partnership, Phoenix, AZ

Unless otherwise noted, Scripture is taken from the NEW AMERICAN STANDARD BIBLE©.
Copyright © 1960, 1962, 1963, 1968, 1971, 1972, 1973, 1975, 1977, 1995, by the Lockman Foundation.
Scripture quotations marked (NIV) are taken from the HOLY BIBLE, NEW INTERNATIONAL VERSION©. NIV©. Copyright © 1973, 1978, 1984 by International Bible Society. All rights reserved.

Readers should be aware that Internet Web sites offered as citations and/or sources for further information may have changed or disappeared between the time this was written and when it was read.

Limit of Liability/Disclaimer of Warranty: While the publishers and authors have used their best efforts in preparing this book, they make no representations or warranties with respect to the accuracy or completeness of the contents of this book and specifically disclaim any implied warranties of representatives of written sales materials. The advice and strategies contained herein may not be suitable for your situation. You should consult with a professional where appropriate. Neither the publishers nor authors shall be liable for any loss of profit or any other commercial damages, including but not limited to special, incidental, consequential, or other damages.

Library of Congress Cataloguing-in-Publication Data
Ashbrook, R, Thomas, and Ted Wueste
Mansions of the Heart Study Guide / R. Thomas Ashbrook and Ted Wueste
Library of Congress Control Number: 2014907720

ISBN 9780991636808
        1. Spiritual Formation.   2. Teresa of Avila, Saint, 1515-1582.
        Moradas. I. Title. 3. Small Group Study

Printed in the United States of America
First Edition

CONTENTS

ACKNOWLEDGMENTS

I (Ted) began taking small groups through *Mansions of the Heart* a few years ago and after leading a few groups I decided to put together a written study guide. The guide consisted of several questions and a spiritual exercise for each chapter. Having something tangible helped participants wrestle with the material and prepare for excellent group reflection. So, I approached Tom about developing something together that could maximize personal reflection and group discussion. To my great joy, Tom agreed.

I (Tom) had been receiving feedback that *Mansions* and it insights had proved life-changing for many and that reading it together proved particularly powerful. While the questions at the end of each Chapter proved helpful, more was needed to help groups explore the depths of their amazing and unique journeys with God. Ted's invitation appeared to be God's invitation, as well. The process of team writing with Ted has been delightful and his experiencing using *Mansions* in a number of groups proved invaluable.

The process of teaming has been a privilege. A deep friendship and bond developed through working together which proved to be the best part of the project. All along the way, it felt so right to be creating in community a piece designed to facilitate community in Christ. We would like to express deep gratitude for all those who contributed to making this study guide a reality. There are many.

I (Ted) would like to thank all the groups at Bethany Bible Church that went through the first groups with the material in its infancy and then the group in Fall 2013 that "beta tested" each chapter as we wrote them. Thanks for all the comments and affirmations. Thanks to Michael Donnelly and Vickie Grantham for edits and suggestions to the manuscript, and to Roy Graham for his creation of the cover art.

I (Tom) acknowledge that any real creative work, if it is to be inspired by the Holy Spirit, must be accomplished in the community of the Holy Spirit. For me, that community begins with my wife Charlotte whose patience and encouragement nourishes my ability to persevere in the hard work of writing. Next, the Order of *Imago Christi*, of which I am a part, brought to bear a vast experience with using the Teresian Mansions as a perspective for coaching Christian leaders. Our collective work together informs many of the questions and approaches that Ted and I put forth in the Study Guide. Thanks for Jeff Sweeny whose editorial eyes helped us immensely. Finally, I want to thanks the dozens of brothers and sisters in Jesus who form the Intercession Team which partners with me in seeking the heart and leading of Jesus.

I (Ted) am grateful to my bride, Jenifer, and my kids, Trey and Claire. They are the loves of my life and they frequently sacrifice so that I can work on projects like this. I know that Father sees and rewards and smiles.

Most of all, we want to thank our beloved Lord, Father, Son, and Holy Spirit, for calling us to this work through which, in some way, He might touch the hearts of many of His beloved with encouragement and strength to joyfully follow Him as He gives us all a new heart in the image of Christ!

INTRODUCTION

Emphasis of the Study Guide

The study guide focuses on your personal experience and attempts to facilitate group discussion which may help shed greater light on your relationship with God. Often, as followers of Christ, we know how to talk a "good game" about information or concepts, but can confuse our knowledge with actually experiencing Him. The questions, exercises, and group discussions in the following chapters provide an opportunity to simply experience Him as we grow in our understanding of how He facilitates our spiritual growth. While this study guide can be used individually, we encourage you to use it with some trusted friends. Scripture encourages us to learn from the Abrahams, Isaacs, and Jacobs, those who have known God in the past as well as our sisters and brothers in Christ today. Our spiritual growth, therefore, happens best in the context of a loving community where God can teach us, not only through the stories of Biblical characters, but also through one another.

Design of the Study Guide

Each chapter of the study guide contains three phases that correspond to three activities we recommend for each week: Reflective Study, Spiritual Exercise, and Group Sharing.

1. We invite you to engage in a time of Reflective Study by yourself. Spend time in prayer. Then take notes as you read the chapter, and record your insights as you study the biblical texts. Finally, reflect on the questions about the chapter content.

2. The Spiritual Exercise, also completed alone, provides an opportunity to engage with God in a way related to the content of each chapter.
3. The Group Sharing guide helps each person explore and share their experiential reflections, providing opportunity to learn from and support one another.

We suggested the following time allotments for the Three Phase Process:

Personal Reflection	approximately 1 hour
Prayer	5-10 minutes
Reading/Notes	varies
Digging deeper	10-20 minutes
Reflection questions	15-30 minutes
Spiritual Exercise	20-30 minutes
Group Discussion	60-75 minutes

The appendices of the study guide provide resources for further study as well as a chart of the mansions for comparison and contrast while reading the chapters.

Suggestions for Group Leaders

Before embarking on this study in a group, we encourage leaders to consider some important perspectives and keep them central in the life of the group.

First, *Mansions of the Heart* provides a great tool for helping us discern our relative place on the journey of our relationship with Jesus, and how God might be at work in us. We need to remember throughout the study that the mansions DO NOT represent stages to be achieved but places or seasons where we abide during our journey with Jesus. Each mansion describes a beautiful place to experience God and His grace in our lives. We attempt to identify the general mansions in which we currently journey, not to try to "measure progress," but to help us better understand our experience of God in that season and participate with God's loving shepherding in our lives. Leaders should watch for and avoid tendencies to compare and strive as participants consider the various mansions.

Second, our spiritual growth is God's work; it's by His grace that we are transformed. However, He invites us to join Him and cooperate in His sanctifying transformation. His work continues, even when we struggle and don't feel like we're growing at all. Although He desires that we join Him in making us Christ-like, He doesn't demand it. He gently and patiently waits until we respond out of love for Him. Leaders should watch for tendencies of participants to try to take responsibility for their own growth by an excessive focus on how to get to the next mansion.

Finally, the depths of relationship with Christ have to be experienced and in many ways can't be objectively explained. Rather than engaging this study with an intellectual focus, see it as an opportunity to experience the greatest Desire of your heart.

Essentials for Group Discussion and Interaction

Select the right place for discussion to provide a safe and confidential environment where participants feel free to share. The "Time Alone with God" in quiet reflection is also a significant part of the group time. A private room in a church or home often works best.

Facilitate the right mode of discussion. Rather than debating the material, participants should seek to understand it in the context of one's experience of God. We certainly don't expect agreement on every thought presented in *Mansions of the Heart*. There may be some things that resonate with some, but not with others. Encourage participants to simply let go of things that don't connect and focus on what the Spirit enlivens within them. While *Mansions* tries hard to connect Teresa's observations to the clear teaching of Scripture, invite participants to investigate the passages for themselves and draw their own biblical conclusions. Each chapter of this study guide includes a section for digging deeper into the biblical text.

Help participants maintain an appropriate spirit of discussion. We encourage one another as we listen attentively and respond. Encourage participants not to interrupt one another. Before we share, we need to prayerfully listen to what God wants us to share. Begin each time of discussion with silent, reflective prayer as everyone seeks to know the Father's heart. Allow for quiet and pauses which can facilitate thought and reflection.

Allow at least one hour for group discussion and interaction. The following general guideline can help you gauge the time needed for each section:

Time with God	5-10 minutes
Review	10-15 minutes
Discussion	30 minutes
Reflection	10 minutes
Prayer	5-10 minutes

While this guideline proposes 60-75 minutes, **utilize a longer group time** to guide the discussion and reflection into those areas that are of most importance for the group. If a longer group time is not possible, utilize smaller groups of 2-3 to engage in the Reflection and Prayer sections in order to allow each person to fully participate and not feel rushed.

Consider how to provide adequate time for the group to share their timelines in Chapter 3. In this chapter, the spiritual exercise encourages writing out a spiritual experience timeline. We've found that sharing our spiritual journey with one another, through these timelines, can be a powerful experience of growth and affirmation. We suggest an extra group meeting or a longer session for Chapter 3.

Facilitate the Time with God section for personal prayer. As a leader, prepare to lead the group in a time of silence, prayer or reflection, depending on the focus of the chapter.

Options for Using this Study Guide
for Group Reflection and Sharing

This study guide provides material for all fourteen chapters of *Mansions of the Heart*, and is therefore easily used for a 14 week study. However, here are some ideas for groups of other durations …

A 6 week study:
Week 1	Chapters 1-3
Week 2	Chapters 4-5
Week 3	Chapters 6-7
Week 4	Chapters 8-9
Week 5	Chapters 10-11
Week 6	Chapters 12-14

A 10 week study:
Week 1	Chapters 1-2
Week 2	Chapters 3
Week 3	Chapters 4-5
Week 4	Chapters 6
Week 5	Chapters 7
Week 6	Chapters 8
Week 7	Chapters 9
Week 8	Chapters 10
Week 9	Chapters 11-12
Week 10	Chapters 13-14

A 12 week study:
Week 1	Chapters 1-2
Week 2	Chapters 3
Week 3	Chapters 4
Week 4	Chapters 5
Week 5	Chapters 6
Week 6	Chapters 7
Week 7	Chapters 8
Week 8	Chapters 9
Week 9	Chapters 10
Week 10	Chapters 11
Week 11	Chapters 12
Week 12	Chapters 13-14

In formats other than a 14-week study, we suggest choosing only one of the "spiritual exercises" in the assigned chapters for that week's reflection. Leaders can use the group format from any of the chapters, but may combine the Content Review questions to cover more material. A longer group time could also be helpful in facilitating fewer sessions.

We (Ted and Tom) pray that the Holy Spirit will use this material to demonstrate His love to you in possibly new and surprising ways. By the very fact that you are reading this book and taking the additional steps of reflective study and discussion, we know that you have a deep longing, as we do, to know more of our Lord and to experience His work in your life more fully. Jesus makes Himself known to those who seek Him as a faithful Shepherd. We encourage you to present yourself to Him in abandoned release, trusting that He is the one who put that longing within you and He will lead you toward its fulfillment. Dare to take Him at His word and join us in the adventure!

... He who enters by the door is a shepherd of the sheep. To him the doorkeeper opens, and the sheep hear his voice, and he calls his own sheep by name and leads them out.... When he puts forth all his own, he goes ahead of them, and the sheep follow him because they know his voice.... I am the door; if anyone enters through Me, he will be saved, and will go in and out and find pasture. I am the good shepherd, and I know My own and My own know Me, even as the Father knows Me and I know the Father; and I lay down My life for the sheep.
John 10:2-4, 9-10, 14-16

CHAPTER 1

IS THIS ALL THERE IS?

Personal Study and Reflection

Time with God

Read the Isaiah 64:8 passage at the beginning of the chapter and spend a few minutes listening to God in the context of this verse. Ask Him to guide your time of reflection and reading.

Notes from the chapter & concepts that connected

Use the space provided to jot down a few notes.

Digging Deeper with the Biblical References

Spend a few minutes reviewing the following passages. In addition, list other Biblical passages that support the concepts of this chapter. (Jot down any insights or questions.)

Ephesians 3:16-19

John 10:7-18

Reflection Questions

1. Recall your "conversion" in becoming a child of God. What tactics and situations did God initially use to get your attention? What does He use most now to draw you closer or get your attention?

2. What metaphor might you use to describe your relationship with God now? How has that metaphor changed over the years?

3. What persons has God used most significantly to guide you into a deepening relationship with Jesus?

4. How are you feeling about your own spiritual growth right now? Backsliding? Stuck? Trudging? Confused? Sailing higher? Other? Record your feelings.

Spiritual Exercise (20 Minutes)

Read Ephesians 1:3-14 reflectively. Putting aside the "foreknew or predestined" controversy for now, consider your own spiritual journey with Jesus. Read each line, one at a time, and then reflect on God's loving process in your own life. It might be helpful to make a list or a simple chart that depicts your journey so far. What feelings emerge as you consider your story as a whole? What do those feelings tell you about yourself and your relationship with God?

Community Discussion and Reflection

Time Alone with God

Pray Ephesians 1:15-23 for yourself. Go slowly through each petition and elaborate on what you feel speaks to your own life experience. What feelings, such as joy, anticipation, fear, resistance, or doubt accompany God's desires for you? What one sentence might express how God is speaking to your particular life situation through this text right now?

Review

How has God been at work in you this week?

What did you notice happening in you while doing the Spiritual Exercise? What did you notice about God and/or yourself as a result of the Spiritual Exercise?

Discussion

Content Review: What spoke to you personally in this introduction to the question of spiritual formation?

Clarifications: What seemed unclear or confusing in the chapter?

Challenges: In what ways was your life with God challenged and/or encouraged by the chapter?

Reflection

What next steps seem to emerge from your reflections in this chapter?

Prayer

How can the group pray for you this coming week about your relationship with God and other life issues? Take a few minutes and pray now. *(If only 5-10 minutes are available, break into groups of 2-3.)*

Additional Notes/Reflections

CHAPTER 2

COMMON MYTHS THAT LEAD DOWN DEAD-END ROADS

Personal Study and Reflection

Time with God

Read the Matthew 7:13-14 passage at the beginning of the chapter and spend a few minutes listening to God in the context of these verses. Ask Him to guide your time of reflection and reading.

Notes from the chapter & concepts that connected

Use the space provided to jot down a few notes.

Digging Deeper with the Biblical References

Spend a few minutes reviewing the following passages. In addition, list other Biblical passages that support the concepts of this chapter. (Jot down any insights or questions.)

Matthew 22:34-40

1 Corinthians 13:1-13

Reflection Questions

1. What "goal" for a relationship with God was encouraged in your spiritual "upbringing?" How has that affected your relationship with God and others over the years?

2. *Mansions of the Heart* describes "holiness" as one of the commonly assumed goals of spiritual formation. What would "holiness" look like in your life? How has that definition changed over the years for you? What eludes you about becoming increasingly holy? When you think of God looking at you from the perspective of holiness, what feeling responses emerge in you?

3. Becoming a 'better worker for God," sometimes called a disciple, represents the goal of spiritual life for many people. What role has "performance" played in your own life motivations? Have your performance standards changed over time? What performance expectations do you think that God might have for you? When you think of God looking at you from the perspective of performance, what feeling responses emerge in you?

4. Personal wholeness and increased knowledge about God also represent primary goals of spiritual growth for some people. To what extent has either of these goals significantly influenced your own motivations? How do you respond to this statement? "A deepening relationship of love is the essential goal of our spiritual formation and that all these 'dead-ends' represent fruits of a relationship of love with God."

Spiritual Exercise (20 Minutes)

Read Ephesians 3:14-19. Move from your reading into a time of quiet reflection and ask God to bring to mind your own history of "love."

1. In what ways has love been fulfilled in your history, particularly as a child? In what ways has love been lacking or betrayed in your experience?

2. Remembering that "love" in these passages refers to the grace filled action of God toward us, how would you rate your "comfort level" as you contemplate a deepening intimacy of love with God?

3. Do you embrace God's invitation or distance yourself from it?

Community Discussion and Reflection

Time Alone with God

As a group, read Ephesians 3:14-19 slowly in a Lectio (a slow repetitive and reflective reading) style and then become still and listen to God's heart and yours. Ask God what He would like to say to you.

Review

How has God been at work in you this week?

What did you notice happening in you while doing the Spiritual Exercise?

Discussion

Content Review: What spoke to you personally in this chapter about the primary goal for your relationship with God?

Clarifications: What appeared unclear or confusing about love as the primary goal?

Challenges: In what ways was your life with God challenged by the chapter?

Reflection

What next steps emerge from your reflections in this chapter?

Prayer

How can the group pray for you this coming week about your relationship with God and other life issues? Take a few minutes and pray now. *(If only 5-10 minutes are available, break into groups of 2-3).*

CHAPTER 3

YOUR JOURNEY INTO THE LOVE OF GOD

Personal Study and Reflection

Time with God

Read the John 14:2-3 passage at the beginning of the chapter, and spend a few minutes listening to God in the context of those verses. Ask Him to guide your time of reflection and reading.

Notes from the chapter & concepts that connected

Use the space provided to jot down a few notes.

Digging Deeper with the Biblical References

Spend a few minutes reviewing the following passages. (Jot down any insights or questions.) In addition, list other Biblical passages that support the concepts of this chapter.

1 John 2:12-13

Ephesians 4:1-16

Reflection Questions

1. Do you find yourself suspicious of the experience of the more mystical elements of faith in Christ? If so, what contributes to that suspicion? If not, how do you view the experiential parts of your faith?

2. Do you generally find perspectives from church traditions other than yours encouraging or disturbing? What criteria do you use to help you discern the helpfulness of aspects of those traditions?

3. How does this introduction to Teresa's model of spiritual growth strike you? What appeals to you and what reservations come to mind?

4. In Teresa's analogy of the Four Waters, which "water" seems to describe your effort in your relationship with Jesus now?

Spiritual Exercise (20 minutes)

Using the Reflection at the end of Chapter 3 in *Mansions of the Heart*, construct a timeline in the space provided below. You may want to use your reflections in the Spiritual Exercise in Chapter 1. After constructing the timeline, reflect upon the ways that God was at work in each situation. Did He seem near/distant/loving? What was your view of Him? What patterns do you see? Record your reflections next to each timeline point.

Community Discussion and Reflection

Time Alone with God

Begin with a few minutes of silence so that everyone can reflect upon which elements of their timelines to share during the personalized group prayer of Psalm 136.

Psalm 136 recounts the history of Israel with the repeated refrain "for His steadfast love endures forever." Steadfast love refers to the initiating, pursuing love of God; love that is consistently active in our lives. As a group, read Psalm 136:1-3. Then, go around the group so that individuals can share episodes from their timeline in a sentence followed by the group reciting "for His steadfast love endures forever."

Pray Psalm 136. Pray and thank God for His faithful love and presence in your life.

Review

How has God been at work in you this week?

What did you notice happening in you while doing the Spiritual Exercise?

Discussion

Content Review:

What is helpful about Teresa's mansion approach as a way to look at the spiritual journey using the analogies of human maturation and the experience of falling in love through getting married? What new insights and encouragements does this give you for your journey?

Clarifications:

What seemed unclear or confusing in the chapter?

Challenges

In what ways did the chapter challenge your life with God?

Reflection

What next steps emerge from your reflections in this chapter?

Prayer

How can the group pray for you this coming week about your relationship with God and other life issues? Take a few minutes and pray now. *(If only 5-10 minutes are available, break into groups of 2-3.)*

Additional Notes/Reflection

CHAPTER 4

NEW BEGINNINGS: THE FIRST MANSION

Personal Study and Reflection

Time with God

Read the Ephesians 2:7-10 passage at the beginning of the chapter and spend a few minutes listening to God in the context of these verses. Ask Him to guide your time of reflection and reading.

Notes from the chapter & concepts that connected

Use the space provided to jot down a few notes.

Digging Deeper with the Biblical References

Spend a few minutes reviewing the following passages. (Jot down any insights or questions.) In addition, list other Biblical passages that support the concepts of this chapter.

1 Corinthians 3:1-3

James 4:1-4

Reflection Questions

1. What experiences highlight your time spent in the first mansion? What was your greatest challenge?

2. A First Mansion motivation was described as "receiving new blessings from God." To what extent has that been a significant motivation for you and what role does it play in your life today?

3. How has your prayer life transitioned from talking to a "God up there" to a "God with me" perspective, and what role does "asking for things" play in your prayer life now?

4. Review the Keys for Growth in the First Mansion. Which spiritual practices have nourished you in the past and how might they still be helpful? Which practices attract you now? Are there any that you feel drawn to explore?

Case Studies

What do you see in Michael's and/or Abigail's story that seems similar to your own experience?

Were there aspects of their experience that seemed unlikely or confusing? Have any of your ideas about the ways in which God works been challenged by what you read?

Did any part of their stories move you emotionally? What do your emotional responses tell you about your relationship with God?

Spiritual Exercise (20 minutes)

Sit quietly and comfortably for a few minutes and ask God to help you become still. Reflectively read Luke 9:23-25 over three times, asking God to speak to you. Pause and rest in God's presence between each reading. Notice a word or phrase that seems to stand out to you. What might God be saying to you? When your mind wanders or thoughts distract you, try repeating the words of Psalm 31:5a. "Into your hands I commit my spirit." Try to stay attentive to God for the full 20 minutes.

Community Discussion and Reflection

Time Alone with God

Ask someone in the group to read Luke 9:23-25 as the rest of the group prayerfully listens and reflects on the words. Allow a few minutes of quiet reflection after the reading.

Review

How has God been at work in you this week?

What did you notice happening in you while doing the Spiritual Exercise?

Discussion

Content Review: What was most significant about your First
                  Mansion experience?

Clarifications: What seemed unclear or confusing in the
                  chapter?

Challenges: In what ways did the chapter challenge your
                  life with God?

Case Studies: How did the stories of Michael and Abigail
                  speak to you?

Reflection

What next steps emerge from your reflections in this chapter?

Prayer

How can the group pray for you this coming week about your relationship with God and other life issues? Take a few minutes and pray now. *(If only 5-10 minutes are available, break into groups of 2-3.)*

CHAPTER 5

BETWEEN A ROCK AND A HARD PLACE: THE SECOND MANSION

Personal Study and Reflection

Time with God

Read Galatians 5:16-17 and spend a few minutes listening to God in the context of these verses. Ask Him to guide your time of reflection and reading.

Notes from the chapter & concepts that connected

Use the space provided to jot down a few notes.

Digging Deeper with the Biblical References

Spend a few minutes reviewing the following passages. (Jot down any insights or questions.) In addition, list other Biblical passages that support the concepts of this chapter.

Galatians 5:16-25

Ephesians 6:10-18

Reflection Questions

1. The movement from the First into the Second Mansion may feel like backsliding. What conflicts between the call of God and the demands of the world have you experienced during this transition? In what ways does the enemy still tempt you with the values and perspectives of this world?

2. As you recall the struggles of your Second Mansion season of growth, how might you have verbalized your longing for your relationship with God? What was the focus of your longing? How would you compare your longing then to your longing today?

3. How did you experience prayer in your Second Mansion season? Did you find it easier or harder to pray than you do now? What was the primary focus of your prayers, and how has that changed?

4. Review the Keys for Growth for the Second Mansion. Which spiritual practices have nourished you in the past and how might they still be helpful? Which practices attract you now? Are there any that you feel drawn to explore?

Case Studies

What do you see in Michael and/or Abigail's story that seems similar to your own experience?

Were there aspects of their experience that seemed unlikely or confusing? Have any of your ideas about the ways in which God works been challenged by what you read?

Did any part of their stories move you emotionally? What do your emotional responses tell you about your relationship with God?

Spiritual Exercise (20 minutes)

Spend some time in John 8:1-11 which shares the story of the woman caught in adultery who was brought to Jesus. As you imagine what the woman must have felt being caught, imagine how the devil might lay a trap to catch you in the secret sins of your life. How would you feel being exposed? After identifying your sins and feelings, imagine Jesus coming to you and responding to you the same way He responded to the woman in the text. What does He say to you? How do you feel? What do you want to do?

Community Discussion and Reflection

Time Alone with God

Begin your time with the following prayer: *Dear Lord, You have told me that I would encounter spiritual warfare as I give myself to love you and walk with you. I am often surprised by the subtle and dangerous schemes of the enemy, and I often fear that I will be overpowered. Help me trust you to defend me and teach me to do warfare in your power.*

Read Ephesians 6:10-17 over slowly, imagining yourself as the warrior described by the apostle Paul. What piece of the 'full armor of God" feels the most difficult for you to put on or use? What does that tell you about your relationship with God and the ways He wants to grow you? How will you respond?

Review

How has God been at work in you this week?

What did you notice happening in you while doing the Spiritual Exercise?

Discussion

Content Review: What spoke to you personally in this chapter about the "rock and hard place" that we experience as we try to live God's way in a world with quite different values?

Clarifications: What seemed unclear or confusing in the chapter?

Challenges: In what ways did the chapter challenge your life with God?

Case Studies: How did the stories of Michael and Abigail speak to you?

Reflection

What next steps emerge from your reflections in this chapter?

Prayer

How can the group pray for you this coming week about your relationship with God and other life issues? Take a few minutes and pray now. *(If only 5-10 minutes are available, break into groups of 2-3.)*

CHAPTER 6

FOLLOWING JESUS: THE THIRD MANSION

Personal Study and Reflection

Time with God

Read Philippians 2:12-13 and spend a few minutes listening to God in the context of these verses. Ask Him to guide your time of reflection and reading.

Notes from the chapter & concepts that connected

Use the space provided to jot down a few notes.

Digging Deeper with the Biblical References

Spend a few minutes reviewing the following passages. (Jot down any insights or questions.) In addition, list other Biblical passages that support the concepts of this chapter.

Ephesians 4:1-3

Philippians 2:12-16

Reflection Questions

1. In the first part of the chapter (p. 92), it is suggested that "the third of the seven mansions is about as far as most churches go in their teaching about the spiritual life. It's an important phase of our growth but many of us get stuck there." In what ways have you felt stuck in your relationship with God?

2. In what ways are you feeling a "holy dissatisfaction" with your spiritual journey? How do the insights of the Third Mansion help you navigate the terrain of your soul?

3. How has journaling or the "ACTS" (Adoration, Confession, Thanksgiving, Supplication) prayer been helpful to you? How might they be an instrumental part of drawing you deeper in Him?

4. Review the Keys for Growth in the Third Mansion. Which spiritual practices have nourished you in the past and how might they still be helpful? Which practices attract you now? Are there any that you feel drawn to explore?

Case Studies

What do you see in Michael and/or Abigail's story that seems similar to your own experience?

Were there aspects of their experience that seemed unlikely or confusing? Have any of your ideas about the ways in which God works been challenged by what you read?

Did any part of their stories move you emotionally? What do your emotional responses tell you about your relationship with God?

Spiritual Exercise (20 minutes)

Spend some time thinking about and pondering the longings of your heart for a deeper relationship with God.

Read Psalm 42:1-2 several times, very slowly … pausing at the end of each phrase. Then, sit quietly and ask the Father to bring your desires for Him into greater focus or clarity.

Repeat your prayer for this longing and sit quietly for 5-10 minutes. As other thoughts surface, simply let them go. If you're distracted by things that need to be done, trust that the Father will bring them back to your mind again later. Whatever thoughts arise, let them go one by one.

As the Father brings your deepest desires for Him to the surface, record them in the space provided.

Take those thoughts and form them into a "longing statement" in the space below:

Community Discussion and Reflection

Time Alone with God

Ask someone in the group to read Psalm 42:1-2 aloud, as the rest of the group prayerfully listens and reflects on the words. Spend a few minutes of quiet reflection after the reading.

Review

How has God been at work in you this week?

What did you notice happening in you while doing the Spiritual Exercise?

Discussion

Content Review: What are the significant joys and frustrations of the Third Mansion season for you?

Clarifications: What seemed unclear or confusing in the chapter?

Challenges: In what ways did the chapter challenge your life with God?

Case Studies: How did the stories of Michael and Abigail speak to you?

Reflection

What next steps emerge from your reflections in this chapter?

Prayer

How can the group pray for you this coming week about your relationship with God and other life issues? Take a few minutes and pray now. *(If only 5-10 minutes are available, break into groups of 2-3.)*

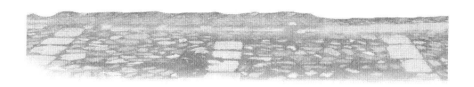

CHAPTER 7

DISCOVERING THE LOVE OF JESUS: THE FOURTH MANSION

Personal Study and Reflection

Time with God

Read the John 21:15 passage at the beginning of the chapter and spend a few minutes listening to God in the context of this verse. Ask Him to guide your time of reflection and reading.

Notes from the chapter & concepts that connected

Use the space provided to jot down a few notes.

Digging Deeper with the Biblical References

Spend a few minutes reviewing the following passages. (Jot down any insights or questions.) In addition, list other Biblical passages that support the concepts of this chapter.

Philippians 3:7-11

John 21:15-17

Reflection Questions

1. In the first paragraph of Chapter 7, the transition to the Fourth Mansion is described as "a subtle transition of huge significance." Describe that transition and how you've experienced it or can imagine experiencing it.

2. How does the longing and desire of one's soul change in the Fourth Mansion? Recalling the "Waters" analogy, how might our understanding of "partnering with God" in our transformation change as we move from the first three mansions and begin exploring the Fourth Mansion?

3. In the Fourth Mansion, prayer transitions from talking to God and takes on more of the dimensions of listening to God in contemplation and meditation. God desires to redirect our prayer life from a focus on self to Him. How does that transition strike you?

4. Review the Keys for Growth in the Fourth Mansion. Which spiritual practices have nourished you in the past and how might they still be helpful? Which practices attract you now? Are there any that you feel drawn to explore?

Case Studies

What do you see in Michael and/or Abigail's story that seems similar to your own experience?

Were there aspects of their experience that seemed unlikely or confusing? Have any of your ideas about the ways in which God works been challenged by what you read?

Did any parts of their stories move you emotionally? What do your emotional responses tell you about your relationship with God?

Spiritual Exercise (20 minutes)

Go on a walk with God in a place where you can focus on the world around you.

Practice the discipline of attentiveness. Simply pray the prayer, "Father, give me eyes to see You." Walk quietly and seek to do nothing but be attentive and aware of His presence in your environment.

If other thoughts or distractions enter your mind, simply let them go as you pray, "Father, I trust You with these thoughts. Give me eyes to see You."

Record your experience in the space provided:

Community Discussion and Reflection

Time Alone with God

Ask someone in the group to read Psalm 46:10-11 aloud. Reflect on the truth of the text that stillness of spirit ushers in a "knowing" or "experiencing" that He is God.

After a reading of these verses slowly and softly, spend several minutes in quiet prayer. Take the following words and silently pray them with pauses between each line.

Be still and know that I am God.
Be still and know that I am.
Be still and know.
Be still.
Be.

Review

How has God been at work in you this week?

What did you notice happening in you while doing the Spiritual Exercise?

Discussion

Content Review:

To what extent have you experienced "falling in love" with Jesus? What has God used to call you into a deeper relationship with Jesus?

Clarifications:

What seemed unclear or confusing in the chapter?

Challenges:

In what ways did the chapter challenge your life with God?

Case Studies:

How did the stories of Michael and Abigail speak to you?

Reflection

What next steps emerge from your reflections in this chapter?

Prayer

How can the group pray for you this coming week about your relationship with God and other life issues? Take a few minutes and pray now. *(If only 5-10 minutes are available, break into groups of 2-3.)*

CHAPTER 8

LONGING FOR ONENESS WITH GOD: THE FIFTH MANSION

Personal Study and Reflection

Time with God

Read the Ephesians 3:17-19 passage at the beginning of the chapter and spend a few minutes listening to God in the context of these verses. Ask Him to guide your time of reflection and reading.

Notes from the chapter & concepts that connected

Use the space provided to jot down a few notes.

Digging Deeper with the Biblical References

Spend a few minutes reviewing the following passages. (Jot down any insights or questions.) In addition, list other Biblical passages that support the concepts of this chapter.

Romans 8:38-39

John 17:20-26

Reflection Questions

1. In your own words and using your experience where applicable, describe the call to move from a focus on discovering a new relationship with Jesus to the desire to fully experience union with God?

2. Deep longing for oneness with God can be accompanied by frustration or dissatisfaction with our seemingly inadequate experience of Him and by our greater awareness of our own sinfulness. How might these frustrations be seen as evidence of deeper growth?

3. How might not "feeling" His presence or struggling to sense His presence in prayer be something that God uses to draw us deeper? How might the enemy use it?

4. Review the Keys for Growth in the Fifth Mansion. Which spiritual practices have nourished you in the past and how might they still be helpful? Which practices attract you now? Are there any that you feel drawn to explore?

5. Can you identify parts of your history that need healing so that you can more fully trust God's love?

Case Studies

What do you see in Michael and/or Abigail's story that seems similar to your own experience?

Were there aspects of their experience that seemed unlikely or confusing? Have any of your ideas about the ways in which God works been challenged by what you read?

Did any part of their stories move you emotionally? What do your emotional responses tell you about your relationship with God?

Spiritual Exercise (20 minutes)

Select a simple verse (that you can repeat from memory) which speaks of your longing for God.

Find a quiet space where you won't be distracted. Set an alarm so that you won't have to worry about the time. Take either ten or twenty minutes and sit with Him. Take the time to just be with Him. Take the first few moments to take a few deep breaths and let go of any distracting thoughts or pressures that are on your mind. Begin to quietly repeat the verse from memory and sit in quiet. As any distracting thoughts arise, just let them move on trusting that He will bring anything necessary back to you as you repeat your verse in your heart.

Use the space provided to record how this time went, being careful not to use positive or negative judgments:

Community Discussion and Reflection

Time Alone with God

Begin with an open time of prayer in which group members pray aloud the verses that were a part of their Spiritual Exercises. After this group prayer, move into a time of silence as each person quietly repeats their verse in their heart.

Review

How has God been at work in you this week?

What did you notice happening in you while doing the Spiritual Exercise?

Discussion

Content Review: How would you describe your longing for God?

Clarifications: What seemed unclear or confusing in the chapter?

Challenges: In what ways did the chapter challenge your life with God?

Case Studies: How did the stories of Michael and Abigail speak to you?

Reflection

What next steps emerge from your reflections in this chapter?

Prayer

How can the group pray for you this coming week about your relationship with God and other life issues? Take a few minutes and pray now. *(If only 5-10 minutes are available, break into groups of 2-3.)*

CHAPTER 9

THE LONG DARK CORRIDOR: THE DARK NIGHTS OF THE SOUL

Personal Study and Reflection

Time with God

Read the Song of Solomon 3:1-2 passage at the beginning of the chapter and spend a few minutes listening to God in the context of these verses. Ask Him to guide your time of reflection and reading.

Notes from the chapter & concepts that connected

Use the space provided to jot down a few notes.

Digging Deeper with the Biblical References

Spend a few minutes reviewing the following passages. (Jot down any insights or questions.) In addition, list other Biblical passages that support the concepts of this chapter.

Psalm 51:3, 8-10

Psalm 42:1-11

Reflection Questions

1. Many places in the Psalms describe personal desolation that didn't seem to be caused by external circumstances. Is that something you have experienced? What did you want from God that He didn't seem to provide at the time?

2. Jesus described in the Sermon on the Mount (Matthew 5:6) that we are blessed when we hunger and thirst for righteousness? How do you feel when you hear that God sometimes hides Himself from us to increase our "hunger and thirst"? How has God used that process to lead you more deeply into relationship with Him?

3. How do you respond when it feels like your prayers "bounce off the ceiling?" How does it feel to sit with God when He doesn't appear to "show up?" What will help you persevere in trust?

4. We read that God brings the Dark Nights when we are strong enough to learn to experience Him beyond our feelings or insights. What resources has God given you to survive that kind of "boot camp" that will make your faith powerful? What additional resources do you need?

Imagining and Remembering

Read the poem "The Dark Night" at the end of Chapter 9. What memories does it evoke? What feelings rise in you (fear, excitement, confusion, etc.)? What prayer emerges within your heart? What does all that tell you about yourself and your walk with God?

Were there parts of the teaching about the Dark Nights in Chapter 9 that seemed unlikely or confusing? How might this challenge some of your ideas about the ways God works and ways He does not?

Spiritual Exercise (20 minutes)

Read 1 Kings 19:1-13 over three times, interspersed by several minutes of silence. Put yourself in Elijah's shoes, but in the context of your present circumstances. Feel what he felt and how it relates to some aspect of your life, now or in the past. How has God offered you bread and water for a journey that would have been too hard for you? How would you answer God when he asks you, "What are you doing here?" What do you need to hear from Him?

Community Discussion and Reflection

Time Alone with God

Prayer: *Jesus, I want to follow You, but when I see that your path lead to the Cross, I become frightened. Help me to trust you and empower me to follow you in faith.*

Read Psalm 23 in the context of your reflection on the 1 Kings 19 passage. Recall times when you experienced each movement of the Psalm. What movement most describes your present experience?

Review

How has God been at work in you this week?

What did you notice happening in you while doing the Spiritual Exercise?

Discussion

Content Review:

What spoke to you personally in this chapter about Dark Nights? How has it informed your experience so far? How do you feel knowing that such times may lay ahead for you? What kind of help will you need to persevere?

Clarifications:

What seemed unclear or confusing in the chapter?

Challenges:

In what ways did the chapter challenge your life with God?

Reflection

What next steps emerge from your reflections in this chapter?

Prayer

How can the group pray for you this coming week about your relationship with God and other life issues? Take a few minutes and pray now. *(If only 5-10 minutes are available, break into groups of 2-3.)*

CHAPTER 10

THE PASSION OF GOD'S LOVE: THE SIXTH MANSION

Personal Study and Reflection

Time with God

Read the Psalm 27:4-6 passage at the beginning of the chapter and spend a few minutes listening to God in the context of these verses. Ask Him to guide your time of reflection and reading.

Notes from the chapter & concepts that connected

Use the space provided to jot down a few notes.

Digging Deeper with the Biblical References

Spend a few minutes reviewing the following passages. (Jot down any insights or questions.) In addition, list other Biblical passages that support the concepts of this chapter.

Psalm 27:4-6

Philippians 3:7-11

Reflection Questions

1. Philippians 3:8 speaks of counting "all things as loss." Where have you experienced the love for God overpower your love for other things? Do you sense His love continuing to lead you in this way?

2. How would you describe the desires of the Sixth Mansions? How have you experienced or tasted those desires? If you're not sure, what do you imagine those desires and longings might look like in your life?

3. In the Sixth Mansion, silent prayer shifts from just being with Him to experiences of His presence. Teresa describes several spiritual experiences in prayer that can emerge during this time. What excites you about this? What concerns you? What resistance do you feel about this kind of relationship with God?

4. Review the Keys for Growth for the Sixth Mansion. What spiritual practices might prove most helpful to you? Teresa says that mentors or spiritual directors are very important during this season of our life with God to help us interpret our experiences of God. Do you have a spiritual director or "spiritual friend" with whom you can discuss and discern the movements of God in your life?

Case Studies

What do you see in Michael and/or Abigail that seems similar to your own experience?

Were there aspects of their experiences that seemed unlikely or confusing? Have any of your ideas about the ways in which God works been challenged by what you've read?

Did any part of their stories move you emotionally? What do your emotional responses tell you about your relationship with God?

Spiritual Exercise

Set aside a full day or half day and do "a day with Jesus." Be attentive to the reality that He is with you each moment, participating in what you do. Find a place where you can minimize distractions and simply enjoy sharing the same space with Jesus.

For example, choose a place where you find it easy to sense God's presence, such as nature, a church, a place with art or music, a place filled with people where you can observe rather than interact. Choose a setting that fits your temperament and supports the ways you experience God most easily. To help you with this exercise, try not to structure your time, but let the Holy Spirit guide you. Simply create the space and let God fill it as He chooses. Don't be afraid of silence, but simply "wait upon the Lord." As much as you may want answers or experiences, surrender fully to God, trusting His loving presence.

What day will you do this?

At the end of the day, record your response to this experience below: (What was it like? What surprised you? What was frustrating?)

Community Discussion and Reflection

Time Alone with God

Prayer: *Jesus, I want to experience Your presence in every situation and moment of my life. Help me grow in my attentiveness to Your presence in all things.*

Set aside a specific amount of time you are able to allot for this exercise. You might want to set a timer so that you are free to be fully present, committing to spend the full time. Read Psalm 131, stilling your soul as the Psalm describes. Spend the rest of the time simply focusing on your presence "in Christ." Let distractions go to His feet, as you remain like a "weaned child." When your timer goes off, thank God for loving you as your heavenly Father with His nurturing, mother-like qualities.

Review

How has God been at work in you this week?

What did you notice happening in you while doing the Spiritual Exercise?

Discussion

Content Review: In thinking about the changing patterns of prayer, what stands out to you about the Sixth Mansion? How do Teresa's "tests for listening" help?

Clarifications: What seemed unclear or confusing in the chapter?

Challenges: In what ways did the chapter challenge your life with God?

Case Studies: How did the stories of Michael and Abigail speak to you?

Reflection

What next steps emerge from your reflections in this chapter?

Prayer

How can the group pray for you this coming week about your relationship with God and other life issues? Take a few minutes and pray now. *(If only 5-10 minutes are available, break into groups of 2-3.)*

CHAPTER 11

A LIFE OF LOVE IN THE TRINITY: THE SEVENTH MANSION

Personal Study and Reflection

Time with God

Read the Song of Solomon 7:10-12 passage at the beginning of the chapter and spend a few minutes listening to God in the context of these verses. Ask Him to guide your time of reflection and reading.

Notes from the chapter & concepts that connected

Use the space provided to jot down a few notes.

Digging Deeper with the Biblical References

Spend a few minutes reviewing the following passages. (Jot down any insights or questions.) In addition, list other Biblical passages that support the concepts of this chapter.

Galatians 2:20

John 17:21-24

Reflection Questions

1. Because not many ever fully live in the Seventh Mansion, use your imagination. What would it be like for you to live in the reality that He fully lives in you? What would it be like to be free from the habitual struggles with sin that plague you? What would it be like to be free to fully enjoy and live out the love of the Trinity?

2. As you consider what you've imagined, how does this connect with your deepest longings? Comparing this longing with an intimate human relationship you've experienced, what does this tell you about what you long for with Jesus?

3. How have you experienced "unintentional self-forgetfulness"? What factors were present in that experience? What might that tell you about growth in the Seventh Mansion?

4. Review the Keys for Growth in the Seventh Mansion. Which spiritual practices have nourished you in the past and how might they still be helpful? Which practices attract you now? Are there any that you feel drawn to explore?

Case Studies

What do you see in Michael and/or Abigail's story that seems similar to your own experience?

Were there aspects of their experience that seemed unlikely or confusing? Have any of your ideas about the ways in which God works been challenged by what you read?

Did any part of their stories move you emotionally? What do your emotional responses tell you about your relationship with God?

Spiritual Exercise (20 minutes)

Read the following passages over slowly three times, giving space for feeling their meaning to you in between the readings: Col 1:25-29, and 2 Cor 5:17-19. The Seventh Mansion represents our fullest possible experience of knowing "Christ in us," and living fully "in Christ." After reading the Scriptures, spend the rest of your time imagining Christ living in you to the extent that you could say with the apostle Paul, "It is not I who live, but Christ who lives in me." Then use your imagination to picture living in Jesus, being part of Him in what He is doing and in His relationship with the Father and the Holy Spirit.

What is God doing in you right now that you can celebrate and for which you can thank Him?

Community Discussion and Reflection

Time Alone with God

Spend a few minutes reviewing the spiritual exercise from this week (specifically the section on what you can celebrate about where He has you in the present moment). Move into a time of silence, followed by a group time of verbally sharing prayers of thanksgiving for what He is doing in the lives of each member of the group.

Review

How has God been at work in you this week?

What did you notice happening in you while doing the Spiritual Exercise?

Discussion

Content Review:
What connects with your heart about Teresa's description of the Seventh Mansion? What does it stir in you?

Clarifications:
What seemed unclear or confusing in the chapter?

Challenges:
In what ways did the chapter challenge your life with God?

Case Studies:
How did the stories of Michael and Abigail speak to you?

Reflection

What next steps emerge from your reflections in this chapter?

Prayer

How can the group pray for you this coming week about your relationship with God and other life issues? Take a few minutes and pray now. *(If only 5-10 minutes are available, break into groups of 2-3.)*

CHAPTER 12

YOUR UNIQUE JOURNEY

Personal Study and Reflection

Time with God

Read the 2 Corinthians 4:7-11passage at the beginning of the chapter and spend a few minutes listening to God in the context of these verses. Ask Him to guide your time of reflection and reading.

Notes from the chapter & concepts that connected

Use the space provided to jot down a few notes.

Digging Deeper with the Biblical References

Spend a few minutes reviewing the following passages. (Jot down any insights or questions.) In addition, list other Biblical passages that support the concepts of this chapter.

Romans 8:19-25

Psalm 139:1-6, 13-16

Reflection Questions

1. What three mansions seem to best describe where you are on your journey?

What excites you about where you are right now?

2. Can you identify wounds or experiences from the past that might still block your growth in your journey with Him?

3. In what ways do you perceive the elements of your temperament to be a challenge for further growth? Do you have any fears related to living and interacting with God the way you are today?

What spiritual disciplines seem to fit your temperament best?

What disciplines, which would seem to stretch you the most, might prove helpful to your growth?

4. Considering the list of potential tools to increase self-knowledge listed in Chapter 12, which seem most appropriate for you now?

Spiritual Exercise (20 Minutes)

Prayerfully sit with God and ask Him the questions below. Sit quietly and listen. Then picture the things He brings to mind.
(*Note: this might be an exercise you complete in several sittings or come back to over a period of several days)

Father, are there any hurts and wounds from my past that you'd like to bring to my attention?

Father, what do you want to say to me about those hurts and wounds?

Father, what do you want to tell me about Yourself related to these parts of my history?

Father, what do you want to tell me about me?

To the extent that it feels appropriate, try praying the following prayer in the context of the situations that God has brought to your attention.

I forgive _____ *(parent, sibling, other person, etc.) for not being a perfect* _____, *and I ask you to forgive them and not hold their sins against them.*

I ask you, Lord, to forgive me for not honoring or loving that person perfectly, and I release any self-condemnation that I may have held relative to this person.

I ask you to heal whatever wounds have been caused in my heart from this experience and to release me to grow into the person you designed me to be. Free me, Lord, to love you fully and to love others as you love me.

Community Discussion and Reflection

Time with God

Reflect on Psalm 139:1-6, 13-16.

Spend a few moments in quiet, simply listening to the words. As the passage is read again slowly, imagine that you are speaking each word to God. Next, spend a few minutes in reflection. What word, picture, or phrase stood out to you? Listen again to these verses being read. What stirs your heart?

Review

How has God been at work in you this week?

What did you notice happening in you while doing the Spiritual Exercise.

Discussion

Content Review: What was most helpful in this chapter?

Clarifications: What seemed unclear or confusing in this chapter?

Challenges: In what ways did this chapter challenge your life with God?

Reflection

What next steps emerge from your reflections in this chapter?

Prayer

How can the group pray for you this coming week about your relationship with God and other life issues? Take a few minutes and pray now. *(If only 5-10 minutes are available, break into groups of 2-3.)*

Additional Notes/Reflections

CHAPTER 13

SPIRITUAL FORMATION
AND THE CHURCH

Personal Study and Reflection

Time with God

Read the Matthew 5:1-6 passage at the beginning of the chapter and spend a few minutes listening to God in the context of these verses. Ask Him to guide your time of reflection and reading.

Notes from the chapter & concepts that connected

Use the space provided to jot down a few notes.

Digging Deeper with the Biblical References

Spend a few minutes reviewing the following passages. (Jot down any insights or questions.) In addition, list other Biblical passages that support the concepts of this chapter.

Ephesians 4:11-32

Hebrews 5:11-14

Reflection Questions

1. What mansion seems most reflected in the preaching and teaching of your church? What aspect of your church life tends to "feed" you and nurture your faith the most?

2. With a general idea about your place in the mansions paradigm, what do you feel would be most helpful to you as part of your church experience? If it doesn't exist, what could you do to either compensate or enable it to come about?

3. How would you describe the perspective of your church leaders about spiritual growth beyond basic discipleship? What can you do to encourage your church leadership as they support the spiritual growth of maturing Christians?

4. This chapter insists that spiritual community is vital for the continued growth of our relationship with God. Describe your spiritual community in this season of your journey, and how might God be calling you to deepen your life in community?

Spiritual Exercise (20 minutes)

Because the Church is the "Body of Christ," Jesus is present and active in every aspect of its life, whether we realize it or not. Try an experiment to see if you can discern His presence and participate with Him in what He is doing. Do a "prayer walk" at church, visiting the locations of ministry functions in which you are involved. If you don't have a Sunday between now and the time your group meets, you might do your walk imaginatively from where you are. Go to the appropriate places and briefly observe what is happening at various times on a Sunday morning and other times during the week. What do you see God doing in that function? Do you see the group relying on His presence, or letting Him sit in the corner, un-noticed? Following your prayer walk and reflections, spend 10 to 15 minutes in silent reflection, attentive to your experience. Listen for what He wants to tell you about YOU. Reflect about how God is inviting you to pray for the people in that activity. In what ways did you see Jesus' presence making a vital difference? What did you learn about how you might cooperate/follow Jesus more specifically?

Community Discussion and Reflection

Time with God

Reflect on your church experience from the perspective of worship. Read Psalm 27 three times, interspersed with a minute of silence between each reading. In the first two readings, reflect on the images of the Psalm and notice which ones stand out to you. In the third reading, listen in the context of your church worship experience. What similarities and distinctions to you recognize? How is God inviting you to experience Him in worship, and what does He expect you to receive from Him alone?

Review

How has God been at work in you this week?

What did you notice happening in you while doing the Spiritual Exercise?

Discussion

Content Review: What spoke to you personally about the
                               church and its role in your spiritual
                               growth in this chapter?

Clarifications: What seemed unclear or confusing in this
                               chapter?

Challenges: In what ways did this chapter challenge
                               your life with God?

Reflection

What next steps emerge from your reflections in this chapter?

Prayer

How can the group pray for you this coming week about your relationship with God and other life issues? Take a few minutes and pray now. *(If only 5-10 minutes are available, break into groups of 2-3.)*

Additional Notes/Reflections

CHAPTER 14

OUR CALL TO ACTION

Personal Study and Reflection

Time with God

Read the Jeremiah 29:11–14 passage at the beginning of the chapter and spend a few minutes listening to God in the context of these verses. Ask Him to guide your time of reflection and reading.

Notes from the chapter & concepts that connected

Use the space provided to jot down a few notes.

Digging Deeper with the Biblical References

Chapter 14 expands the discussion beyond the personal spiritual journey of our First Order Calling to love God to address our Second Order Calling to love our neighbor. Spend a few minutes reviewing the following passages. (Jot down any insights or questions.)

In addition, list other Biblical passages that support the concepts of this chapter.

Luke 10:25-17

1 John 4:19-21

Reflection Questions

1. In reflection on your journey with Jesus, how have you noticed the relationship between the depth of your relationship with Him and your ability to follow Him in everyday life?

2. In light of your discoveries about your own journey into the love of God and your place in that journey from a mansions perspective, how might God be calling you to help other believers grow in their love relationship with God?

3. As you picture your various roles in family and society, apart from church programs, how might Jesus want to make His presence in you known to others?

4. Sociologists tell us that "religion" as we have known it is in the midst of massive change. People recognize within themselves a huge "hunger and thirst" for an authentic spiritual life, a life in the love of God described by the New Testament. Jesus says that they shall be satisfied. Recall your own history of hunger and thirst. What has Jesus used most to satisfy you, and what might that say about how He is calling you to be a "bearer of good news" to others on the journey?

Spiritual Exercise (20 minutes)

Read Revelation 21:1-8 in a slow and repetitive manner the way we have done throughout this study. Use your imagination to picture the new heaven and earth where the fullness of the love of God is experienced. Then imagine those you know who might be described by verse 8. Ask the Holy Spirit to show you the heart of the Father and of Jesus in these times. What is God feeling? What are you feeling? What is the Holy Spirit saying to you?

Community Discussion and Reflection

Time Alone with God

Dearest Jesus, help me to live in your love and to follow you as you long for others to know your love. Strengthen me to be a light in this dark world.

Read Isaiah 6: 1-8 over reflectively. Consider the ways that God has revealed Himself to you over the years, forgiven your sin, and healed you. Imagine yourself standing before God and responding as Isaiah did. What is God calling you to do? How does that make you feel? Can you trust Him with the mission?

Review

How has God been at work in you this week?

What did you notice happening in you while doing the Spiritual Exercise?

Discussion

Content Review: What spoke to you personally in this chapter about God's call to action both in our own spiritual formation and in helping the Christian family grow into the likeness of Christ?

Clarifications: What seemed unclear or confusing in this chapter?

Challenges: In what ways did this chapter challenge your life with God?

Reflection

What next steps emerge from your reflections in this chapter?

Prayer

How can the group pray for you this coming week about your relationship with God and other life issues? Take a few minutes and pray now. *(If only 5-10 minutes are available, break into groups of 2-3.)*

APPENDICES

Appendix A: Going Deeper – An Annotated Bibliography

Imago Christi Annotated Reading List[1]

Sometimes what may be obvious is important enough to point out again and again: The Bible is our primary text and guide in this life of the Spirit in Christ.

There is the perennial temptation to substitute reading about prayer for praying. For all its merits, reading about prayer can keep us at the point of simply speculating about prayer. Increasing one's knowledge about prayer is only of real benefit if it is applied by creating space internally in our hearts and externally in our circumstances to pray.

About spiritual books, Emilie Griffin remarked: "Books are sometimes a better help than friends in a commitment to take prayer seriously. In fact, books are friends and supporters in that effort, spiritual partners of a sort." We think so too, and offer this Reading List in the hopes that you will make some new friends.

Part I
General Spiritual Formation and Prayer

Arintero, John G. *The Mystical Evolution in the Development and Vitality of the Church*. Rockford, IL: Tan Books and Publishers, Inc., 1978.

This is a Catholic "encyclopedia" of spiritual growth in individuals and the church. While it is definitely Roman Catholic in perspective, it is a good resource for discussion of historical spiritual subjects.

---

[1] Used by Permission from The Order of *Imago Christi:* See www.ImagoChristi.org

Boa, Kenneth. *Conformed to His Image: Biblical and Practical Approaches to Spiritual Formation.* Grand Rapids, MI: Zondervan Publishing House, 2001.

Boa develops 12 "facets" of Christian spirituality and provides an excellent overview of an evangelical perspective of spiritual formation.

Calhoun, Adele, *Spiritual Disciplines Handbook: Practices That Transform Us.* Westmont, IL: InterVarsity Press, 2005

Collins, Kenneth J. *Exploring Christian Spirituality: An Ecumenical Reader.* Grand Rapids, MI: Baker Books, 2000.

Gives a good overview of various spiritual traditions in light of an evangelical perspective.

Coombs, Marie Theresa, and Hermit and Francis Kelley Nemeck. *The Spiritual Journey: Critical Thresholds and Stages of Adult Spiritual Genesis.* Wilmington, DE: Michael Glazier Books, 1987.

A good early work in looking at stages of spiritual growth related to the Teresian mansions. It is a technical work and does a good job of comparing views of spiritual growth among several authors.

Foster, Richard J. *Celebration of Discipline.* San Francisco, CA: Harper & Row, 1988.

This is Foster's classic work in making the classical spiritual disciplines understandable to evangelicals. The spiritual disciplines certainly transcend all the Teresian Mansions, and will certainly be used differently as one moves forward in increasing intimacy with the Trinity.

_____. *Prayer; Finding the Heart's True Home.* San Francisco, CA: HarperSanFrancisco, 1992.

This work is an excellent call to prayer and introduces meditative and contemplative prayer to the evangelical audience.

―――――. *Streams of Living Water: Celebrating the Great Traditions of Christian Faith.* San Francisco, CA: Harper Collins, 1998.

Foster makes the case for receiving insight in our spiritual journey from the various streams of Christian tradition, showing that there are legitimate influences from each. The "streams" are somewhat arbitrary and stereotypical, but helpful and insightful.

Griffin, Emilie. *Clinging: The Experience of Prayer.*

A wonderfully written book about the believer's attachment to God we call prayer. It may serve as a catalyst to prayer as the author discloses several of the movements of the soul in this relationship of trust.

Hagberg, Janet A. and Robert Guelich. *The Critical Journey: Stages in the Life of Faith.* Salem, WI: Sheffield, 1989.

The authors make an attempt at a spiritual formation paradigm that describes the full range of the Christian life. It, however, based upon their personal observations and experiences and has no historical grounding. Nevertheless, there are some important insights, such as the "wall" in Chapter 7.

Howard, Evan B. *Affirming the Touch of God: A Psychological and Philosophical Exploration of Christian Discernment,* Lanham, NY: University Press of America, 2000.

Evan has been a spiritual formation advisor for InnerCHANGE, a division of Church Resource Ministries, for some years. His work is helpful in looking at Christian discernment and for his history of spirituality.

Jung, Carl. *Psychological Types.* New York, NY: Harcourt, Brace. 1923.

Jung provides the foundational psychology for the Myers-Briggs Type Indicator. Important reading if one wants to really understand Myers-Briggs.

May, Gerald G. *The Awakened Heart: Opening Yourself to the Love You Need.* San Francisco, CA: Harper Collins, 1991.

May helps to identify and orient the inner journey of the heart (prayer) in the larger context of one's life and one's living. As the title suggests, the author leads his reader to explore their capacity to love and to be loved.

Mass, Robin, and Gabriel O'Donnell, O.P. *Spiritual Traditions for the Contemporary Church.* Nashville, TN: Abington Press, 1990.

Mass and O'Donnell provide a good overview of spiritual traditions in the church.

Myers, Isabel Briggs and Mary McCaulley. *Manual: A Guide to the Development and Use of the Myers-Briggs Type Indicator.* Palo Alto, CA: Consulting Psychologists Press, 1985.

This is the basic manual on the use of the Meyers-Briggs.

Michael, Chester and Marie Norrisey. *Prayer and Temperament.* Charlottesville, VA: Open Door Press, 1984.

For those familiar with Myers-Brigg's temperament analysis, and who are wanting to get out of a dry prayer rut, or explore a variety of approaches in prayer, Michael and Norrisey's book provides a way to discover what style of prayer is best for you. You do not need to know your type, nor be well-versed in Myers-Brigg's, but the more familiar you are with it, the more you'll get out of this study and practice. The book and research is done from a Catholic perspective, but the temperament insights and "prayer suggestions" at the end of chapters 3-7 are extremely useful exercises for those trying to expand their horizons in prayer.

Mulholland, Jr., Robert M. *Invitation to a Journey: A Road Map for Spiritual Formation.* Downers Grove, IL: InterVarsity Press, 1993.

Invitation provides a good overview of spiritual formation that puts conformity to the image of Christ at the center of the spiritual formation process. Watch, though, that Mulholland tends to make it a means to another end as he adds, "for the sake of others," on the end of his spiritual formation definition. Mulholland also provides an excellent evangelical explanation of "spiritual reading" (*Lectio Divina* in ch. 9). A careful application of this prayer method solidly grounds our experience of God in the Scriptures, providing a foundation for contemplative prayer.

Murray, Andrew. *The Prayer Life.* Whitaker House

Murray's books on prayer are classics. This one offers biblical instruction and exhortation beginning with the struggle of prayerlessness and moves to build a foundation for a life of prayer.

Toon, Peter. *Meditating as a Christian.* Glasgow, Great Britain: Collins, 1991.

Toon gives a useful contribution to the subject from an evangelical Episcopal perspective.

Tugwell, Simon. *Prayer: Living With God.* Springfield, IL: Templegate Publishers, 1975.

This book works as a summons to prayer: succinct, direct and engaging. The author, a Catholic, draws on many sources throughout the history of the Church.

Underhill, Evelyn. *The Spiritual Life.* Harrisburg, PA: Morehouse Publishing, 1955.

Underhill explores the spiritual life as communion with God.

Westerhoff, John. *Spiritual Life: Foundation for Preaching and Teaching.* Louisville, KY: Westminster John Knox Press, 1994.

Westerhoff provides good identification of the basic classical view of spiritual formation and the call for preachers and teachers to ground their ministry in their relationship with Christ.

Part II

Having reference to the Teresian Mansions

Teresa of Ávila. *Interior Castle.* Tr. E. Allison Peers. New York, NY: Doubleday, 1972.

Ashbrook, R. Thomas. *Mansions or the Heart: Exploring the Seven Stages of Spiritual Growth:* San Francisco, CA:, Jossey-Bass, 2009.

> *Mansions* was written for anyone who wants to develop a deeper more meaningful relationship with God. *Mansions of the Heart* offers a step-by-step guide through a spiritual formation road map based on Teresa of Avila's Seven Mansions. The book will help you discern your place on your spiritual journey and offers church leaders a process for helping church members to grow into spiritual maturity.

Dubay, Thomas. *Fire Within. St. Teresa of Avila, St. John of the Cross, and the Gospel on Prayer.* San Francisco, CA; Ignatius Press, 1989.

> This is an excellent overview of Teresa of Avila and John of the Cross relative to spiritual formation.

Last on the List, but First in Priority and Authority:

The New American Standard Bible, Nashville, TN: Thomas Nelson Publishers, 1978

> It might seem superfluous to mention the Bible in any one Mansion, as God's written Word is essential to our entire Christian experience. However, in the latter Mansions, the Scriptures take on a new dimension of allowing the believer to simply "be with" our Lord in both His immanence and

transcendence. While many of the "how to" books are no longer needed, the inspired word of God is a blessed participation in the Father who authored it, with the Son who fulfilled it, and with the Holy Spirit who breathed it then and now.

The Fourth Mansion

Allender, Dan B. and Tremper Longman, III, *The Cry of the Soul: How Our Emotions Reveal Our Deepest Questions About God.* Colorado Springs, CO: Navpress, 1994.

As love for God becomes more of a core motivation, our emotional responses are more important to recognize and understand. This work explores healthy and unhealthy responses.

Augustine, *The Confessions,* Trans. Hal M. Helms, Orleans, MA: Paraclete Press, 1986.

Classical look at the spiritual formation of one of history's greatest fathers.

Barth, Karl. *The Epistle to the Romans.* New York, NY: Oxford University Press, 1968.

Some excellent reading as it relates to relational theology and a love relationship with the Trinity as the goal of spiritual formation.

Bonaventure. *The Soul's Journey into God, The Tree of Life and The Life of St. Francis.* London, England: SPCK, 1978.

Bonaventure provides a great devotional reading in short sections about the spiritual journey.

Bondi, Roberta C. *To Love as God Loves: Conversations with the Early Church.* Philadelphia, PA: Fortress Press, 1987.

Bondi provides an excellent work examining what it means to love and be loved by God. The author carries on this dialogue with writers in the early church, so it is also an excellent overview of key voices about the love of God and how His nature expresses itself in our lives.

Edwards, Gene. *The Divine Romance.* Wheaton, IL: Tyndale House, 1992.

A story rendition of the love relationship with Christ.

Guyon, Jeanne. *Experiencing the Depths of Jesus* Christ. Auburn, Maine: The Seed Sowers, 1975.

This readable version of Madame Guyon's classic sparked a spiritual revival in 18th century France. Convinced that the depths of contemplation are for everyone, Those familiar with contemplative prayer will find Guyon's descriptions of the inward journey very helpful as well.

Hansen, David. *Long Wandering Prayer: An Invitation to Walk with God,* Downers Grove, Il: InterVarsity Press, 2001.

Hansen addresses the subject of hunger for prayer that goes beyond the traditional devotional time of most "discipled" Christians. While not really addressing contemplation, he proposes interactive communication and reflection through walking and activity.

Hazard, David. *Rekindling the Inner Fire Devotional Series,* Minneapolis, MN: Bethany House Publishers, 1991- 1995.

This is an excellent devotional series that exposes the reader to historic mystic writers, along with a good introduction to the writers themselves. Listed in the Fourth Mansions here, but the readings are good throughout.

Hettinga, Jan David. *Follow Me: Experience the Loving Leadership of Jesus,* Colorado Springs, CO: Navpress, 1996.

This work, edited by Dallas Willard is a call into the Fourth Mansion, although not by that name. It is helpful in distinguishing the leadership of the world and the leadership of Jesus that leads into a relationship of love.

Houston, James M. *A Life of Prayer; Faith and Passion for God Alone,* Minneapolis, MN: Bethany House, 1983, 1998.

Part of the Classics of Faith and Devotion Series. Selected writings from Teresa of Avila on prayer and its relationship to spiritual growth.

Huggett, Joyce. *The Joy of Listening to God: Hearing the Many Ways God Speaks to Us.* Downers Grove, IL: InterVarsity Press, 1986.

The best primer on listening prayer for the evangelical that I have read. The author is faithfully evangelical in her perspective but does not sidetrack the importance of meditation and contemplation.

Lawrence, Brother, *The Practice of the Presence of God,* trans. Robert J. Edmondson, Orleans, MA: Paraclete Press, 1985.

A classic work that illustrates complete devotion to a life of faith in love with God.

Lewis, C. S. *Mere Christianity: Beyond Personality: First Steps in the Doctrine of the Trinity.* Bles, 1944. Macmillan, 1945. Paper: In *Mere Christianity*, Macmillan. Included in the Great Books, 1968.

In Book IV of this classic apologetic work, Lewis presents the case for essential Christianity belief, the only goal of which is the complete transformation of the believer by participation in the life of the Trinity. While his purpose is clearly evangelistic, the presentation of the life and love of the Triune God as the source, the means and the goal of the Christian life inspires a longing for the "good infection" to take hold of their lives.

————. *The Screwtape Letters.* New York, NY: Macmillan, 1943.

An important work for understanding the schemes of the devil toward spiritually maturing Christians.

————. *The Great Divorce.* New York, NY: Simon & Schuster, 1946.

Profound insights into the dynamics of sin and grace in our lives.

Manning, Brennan. *Abba's Child.* Wheaton, IL: Tyndale House, 1998.

Each of Manning's books is helpful in looking at our lives in the context of God's radical love and discovering the freedom of that life.

————. *The Ragamuffin Gospel,* Sisters, OR: Multnomah. Pub, 1990.

————. *Ruthless Trust.* San Francisco, CA: HarperCollins, 2000.

————. *Wisdom of Tenderness: What Happens When God's Fierce Mercy Transforms Our Lives.* San Francisco, CA: HarperCollins, 2002.

Martin, Ralph. *Hungry for God: Practical Help in Personal Prayer.* Garden City, NY: Doubleday, 1974

Martin provides a good overview on prayer for the person called into deeper intimacy with God. The work gives an excellent correlation with the Charismatic experience.

Murray, Andrew. *Waiting on God.* Kensington Place, PA: Whitaker House, 1981, 1998.

In the Foreword the author writes that he has come to see that the deepest truth concerning the Christian's relationship to God is to be centered in waiting on Him. Meditations on the subject follow, leaving the impression it is a book that has been prayed into being.

McDowell, Nancy. *Thirsting for God: Encountering God through Abiding Prayer*, 2006.

This powerful small group material, along with a leader's guide is available from the *Imago Christi* website www.imagochristi.org. Using material from the Ignatian Exercises, this resource helps to develop a safe place for believers at any stage to experience the wonders of Abiding Prayer. Nancy is a Core Member of Imago Christi, a certified spiritual director, and has presented at the Spiritual Formation Discovery for Leaders. To order, go to www.imagochristi.org.

Nouwen, Henri J. M. *Life of the Beloved*. New York, NY: Crossroads, 1996.

Nouwen provides a devotional work focusing on a love relationship with God.

_____. *The Genesee Diary: Report from a Trappist Monastery*. Garden City, NY: Image Books, 1976.

Nouwen provides a devotional guide focusing on the themes of the mystical life.

_____. *The Inner Voice of Love: A Journey Through Anguish to Freedom*, New York, NY: Doubleday, 1996.

This is Nouwen's diary through some very difficult years, whose anguish was necessary for Nouwen to find a life of real freedom. The nature and reality of dispassion (The Desert Fathers) or indifference (Ignatius) is seen in the context of human relationships.

_____. *The Only Necessary Thing, Living a Prayerful Life*, New York, NY: Crossroads, 1999.

This is a helpful reminder of the basic principles of living the life of loving relationship with God and maintaining a life of prayer that responds to that relationship.

_____. *The Way of the Heart,* New York, NY: Ballantine Books, 1981.

Nowen describes a simple introduction to Christian contemplation as a way of experiencing the love of God.

Smith, Hannah Whitall. *The Christian's Secret of a Happy Life.* Old Tappan, NJ: Fleming H Revell Co., 1979.

Smith provides a great work on the life of faith for one who is looking for a guide on how to live relationship with Christ to the fullest.

The Interior Life, (by a Carthusian), Paraclete Series, Cork, UK: Cecil Paul Hurwitz Publications, 1951.

This is a basic work on the life of prayer and devotion in silence, from the Cistercian perspective.

Thomas, Gary. *Seeking the Face of God: The Path to a More Intimate Relationship with Him,* Eugene, OR: Harvest House, 1994.

Thomas provides a good overview of the spiritual life for those entering into a life focused on love for God and interactive prayer.

Tozer, A. W. *The Pursuit of God.* Harrisburg, PA: Christian Publications, 1948.

This self-studied preacher steeped in classical works of Christian spirituality makes a desperate plea for evangelicals to "follow hard after God" ... to begin "the glorious pursuit, the heart's happy exploration of the infinite riches of the Godhead." Tozer dissects the ills that keep us from the deeper life and points the way towards developing greater sensibility and receptivity to God's Presence.

Urs Von Balthasar, Hans. *Prayer.* Tr. Graham Harrison. San Francisco, CA: Ignatius Press, 1955.

The author, a notable European Roman Catholic theologian of the past century, offers a theological and philosophical examination of contemplative prayer that is second to none. It is a work steeped in Catholic perspectives, but it is a rich source for those who like to mine truth. This work has relevance in Mansions 4-7.

Wakefield, James, *Sacred Listening: Discovering the Spiritual Exercises of Ignatius.* Grand Rapids MI, Baker Books, 2006.

An evangelical adaptation of the Spiritual Exercises of St. Ignatius of Loyola. These 24 weeks/units have been taken from the 19th annotation of the Exercises.

Weatherhead, Leslie D. *The Will of God,* Nashville, TN, Abington Press, 1954.

This work is foundational for those entering into the prayer of discernment with a real desire to follow Christ in all things, understanding that the different levels of the will of God are important.

Willard, Dallas. *In Search of Guidance: Developing a Conversational Relationship with God.* San Francisco, CA: Harper & Row, 1984.

Willard looks at the nature of prayer and the need for it to be two-way.

———. *The Spirit of the Disciplines: Understanding How God Changes Lives.* San Francisco, CA: Harper & Row, 1988.

The theological foundations underlying Richard Foster's *Celebration of Discipline.*

The Fifth Mansion

Bernard of Clairvaux. *On The Song of Songs.* Cistercian Fathers Series, Kilian J. Walsh, and Irene M. Edmonds, ed. vol. 40. Spencer, MA: Cistercian Publications, 1971-1980.

Bernard has created an important work on understanding life in the love of God and responding to that love.

————.*The Love of God.* Portland, OR: Multnomah Press, 1983.

Another great work for one who is being called into a life of love in God.

Eckhart, Johannes, *Meister Eckhart: Selected Writings,* (Penguin Classics), London, UK: Penguin Books, 1994.

This work provides great insights into Christian mysticism.

Edwards, Gene, *A Tale of Three Kings: A study in Brokenness,* Wheaton, IL, Tyndale House, 1980.

An important insight into the betrayal and brokenness that happens to Christians attempting to live as faithful followers of Jesus and how He uses our brokenness to conform us to His image.

Englebert, Omer, *St. Francis of Assisi,* Ann Arbor, MI: Servant Books, 1965.

The author provides a good introduction to the life of St. Francis as a model for one attempting to live a life totally devoted to Christ.

Guinness, Os. *The Call; Finding and Fulfilling the Central Purpose of Your Life,* Nashville, TN: Word Publishing, 1998.

The author provides a significant work that suggests how Christians might live life totally based upon God's foundational call on their lives. It is a good work for the Fifth Mansions Christian who is working out the details of total devotion. It is also applicable for earlier mansions.

Houston, James. *The Mentored Life: From Individualism to Personhood.* Colorado Springs, CO: NavPress, 2002.

A significant theological and practical work addressing our need to live in relationship.

Kavanaugh, Kieran, and Otilio Rodriguez. *The Collected Works of St. Teresa of Avila.* Washington DC: ICS Publications, 1986.

Not easy reading, but profound, by one of the most influential writers on the spiritual life and prayer.

————. *The Collected Works of St. John of the Cross.* Washington DC: ICS Publications, 1987.

St. John shares his complex paradigm for spiritual formation. He is best known for his insights into the Dark Nights. The work is significant for those entering the 5th through 7th mansions.

Main, John, *Word into Silence,* New York, NY: Paulist Press, 1981.

An excellent introduction into the realm of silence in prayer.

Merton, Thomas, *Contemplative Prayer,* Garden City, NY: Image Books, 1971.

Merton provides a classic work on the method of contemplation. The reader may need to dismiss some references which do not fit evangelical language and theology.

————. *Spiritual Direction and Meditation & What is Contemplation?* Wheathampstead-Hertfordshire: Anthony Clark, 1975.

In this collection of booklets, the Trappist monk speaks to the heart of each of these matters and speaks clearly of the truths and practices, that are crucial for further growth into the "infused mansions." While speaking particularly to people from his tradition, Merton writes in a concise manner palatable for all Christians.

Pennington, Basil. *Centering Prayer.* New York, NY: Image Books, 1982.

A classic work on the method of contemplation. The reader may need to dismiss some references which do not fit evangelical language so as not to miss the historic and important insights.

Palmer, G.E.H., Phillip Sherrard, and Kallistos Ware, ed. *The Philokalia - The Complete Text. Translated by St. Nikodimos of the Holy Mountain & St. Makarios of Corinth.* Vol. 1-4, London/Boston, MA: Faber and Faber, 1979-1984.

The entire work is foundational for understanding the roots of the mystical life and the prayer of the heart and silence. Evagrios, in Volume 1 is particularly important in understanding infused contemplation and spiritual warfare in prayer. Peter of Damascus, in Volume 2 is also very helpful in understanding personal holiness and struggles in prayer.

Russell, Norman. *The Lives of the Desert Fathers: The Historia Monachorum in Aegypto.* Kalamazoo, MI: Cistercian Publications, 1980.

The author provides a classic work detailing accounts of the early Desert Fathers in Northern Africa.

Sandford, John and Paula. *The Transformation of the Inner Man.* Tulsa, OK: Victory House, Inc., 1982.

Sandford gives an excellent in depth look at the spiritual healing that underlies all emotional and bodily health. Its provides a great overview and Biblical background along with in depth examples of common wounds that block our spiritual growth.

Sanford, Agnes. *The Healing Gifts of the Spirit.* Old Tappan, NJ: Fleming H. Revell Company, 1966.

Among many of the author's works, this book provides her best foundational work outlining the biblical truths and practical approaches to experiencing Christ's healing for the physical, emotional, and spiritual wounds that torment out lives.

Seamonds, David A. *Healing for Damaged Emotions.* Wheaton, IL: Victor Books, 1981.

The author provides a helpful perspective for spiritual healing that underlie emotional issues.

Shannon, William H., *Silence on Fire: Prayer of Awareness*, New York, NY, Crossroads Publishing, 1991, 2000.

Silence on Fire is an excellent work about the foundations and nature of responsive prayer in an expansion of the work of Thomas Merton. The work focuses particularly on the importance of our awareness of the presence of God. It includes many useful analogies and example.

Smedes, Lewis. *Shame and Grace: Healing the Shame We Don't Deserve.* San Francisco, CA: Harper San Francisco, 1993.

Smedes provides important insights into the shame based society and religion in which many Christians were raised.

The Way of the Pilgrim and the Pilgrim Continues His Way. Unknown Author, Translated by Helen Bacavcin: Garden City, NY: Image Books, 1978.

This work describes the journey of a Russian pilgrim that introduces the Jesus Prayer and the Philokalia. Wonderful for insight into detachment and the prayer of the heart.

Wigglesworth, Smith. *Ever Increasing Faith.* Springfield, MO: Gospel Publishing House, 1924.

This work describes the story of one of our greatest evangelists who struggles to live the intimate life amidst the passion of bringing others to Christ.

Willard, Dallas. *The Divine Conspiracy: Rediscovering Our Hidden Life in God.* San Francisco, CA: Harper & Row, 1998.

Willard gives a theological and prophetic call to the church about our need for spiritual formation.

———. *Renovation of the Heart: Putting On the Character of Christ.* Colorado Springs, CO: NavPress, 2002.

This is Willard's overview of spiritual formation. It is important for understanding the most influential spiritual formation writings for evangelicals. Like many other works, a love relationship with God, comes very close to becoming simply a by-product of a greater purpose.

Writings from the Philokalia On Prayer of the Heart, (Translated from the Russian Text "Dobrotolubie") trans. E. Kadloubovsky and G.E.H. Palmer, London, UK: Faber and Faber, 1951.

While not the full Philokalia, the writings are useful for devotional texts leading to contemplation and reflections on spiritual warfare.

The Sixth Mansion

Cummings, Charles. *Spirituality and the Desert Experience.* Denville NJ: Dimension Books, 1978.

Fr. Cummings, one of the monks at Holy Trinity Abbey in Huntsville, Utah, gives a very helpful understanding of the "desert" experience in prayer from a Cistercian perspective.

De Caussade, Jean-Pierre. *The Sacrament of the Present Moment.* (Translated by Kitty Muggeridge from the original text of "Self Abandonment to Divine Providence), San Francisco, CA: Harper and Row, 1966.

This work provides devotional reading that focuses on experiencing the Trinity in the present as a way of experiencing the transcendent.

De Sales, Francis. *Introduction to the Devout Life,* trans. John K. Ryan, New York, NY: Doubleday, 1950.

This work provides devotional reading and exercises focusing on faithfulness to the love of God.

Johnson, Darrell W. *Experiencing the Trinity,* Vancouver, BC: Regent College Publishing, 2002.

Johnson addresses Trinitarian theology as the heart of biblical Christianity and the center of Christian experience.

Moltmann, Jurgen. *Trinity and the Kingdom: The Doctrine of God.* San Francisco, CA: Harper & Row, 1981.

The author provides a good theological work on the Trinity as the basis for understanding our relationship with Christ and our spiritual formation.

Nesser, Joann. *Journey into Reality through Prayer and God-Centeredness.* Prior Lake, MN: Living Waters, 1998.

_____. *Prayer: Journey From Self to God.* Lino Lakes, MN: Christos Center for Spiritual Formation, 1985.

Both works provide good foundational insights on prayer as a path to deepening intimacy with God.

Origen. *Origen.* Translated by Rowan A. Greer. New York, NY: Paulist Press, 1979.

Origin's insights are important for understanding much of the thinking that formed the world view of the early church.

Talbot, John Michael. *The Lover and the Beloved: A way of Franciscan Prayer.* New York, NY: Crossroad Publishing Company, 1985.

Talbot shares a wonderful look at our growing relationship with Christ through the analogy of Bride and Bridegroom.

The Cloud of Unknowing and the Letter of Private Direction, trans. Robert Way. Trabuco Canyon, CA: Source Books, 1986

The Cloud is a classic for understanding about what it is to "know God" apart from the senses and the intellect. It is a foundational description of the apophatic approach.

Underhill, Evelyn. *Mysticism: A Study in the Nature and Development of Man's Spiritual Consciousness.* London, England: Methuen & Co. Ltd., 1911.

This noted authority explains in simple, direct language how the practice of mysticism can raise spiritual consciousness, resulting in a better grasp of reality, improvements in efficiency and problem-solving skills, as well as a better reconciliation of duties and ideals to the ordinary demands of daily existence.

————. *Abba.* Harrisburg, PA: Morehouse Publishing, 1982.

> A classic work of rediscovery of the intimate nature of the relationship with God to which we are called.

————. *The Mystical Way: A Psychological Study in Christian Origins.* London, England: J.M. Dent & Sons, 1993.

Tuoti, Frank X. *Why Not Be a Mystic?* New York, NY: Crossroad, 2000

> Looks at the mystical life from a modern day perspective.

The Seventh Mansion

St. Athanasius, *On the Incarnation,* Crestwood, NY: ST. Vladimir's Theological Seminary, 1946.

> This is a foundational work on Trinitarian Theology and an important perspective for those experiencing the Trinity.

Boniface, Archimandrite, *Eastern Monasticism and the Future of the Church,* Stamford, CT: Basileos Press, 1993.

> This work investigates the "Code of Canons for the Oriental Churches, particularly Title XII, "On Monks and Other Religious." It gives good insight into the significance of the Orthodox contribution to the Church.

Chambers, Oswald, *My Utmost for His Highest,* New York, NY: Dodd, Mead and Co, 1935.

> While Oswald Chambers has been a favorite devotional writer for people in Mansions Three through Seven, it is listed here for Chambers' mystical profundity.

De Caussade, Jean-Pierre, *Abandonment to Divine Providence,* New York, NY: Doubleday, 1966.

> This work provides important insights for living a life of

holiness. It brings experience of God out into the open terrain of the living, instructing the reader how to be deeply present to God at any time in any place.

Fenelon, Francois de Salignac de La Mothe. *Let Go*. Springfield, PA, Whitaker House, 1973.

This is a series of letters written to directees in France in the seventeenth century, providing a wonderful encouragement that challenges us to live a faithful life in the midst of modern culture.

The Letters of Saint Anthony the Great, Trans Derwas J. Chitty, Fairacres Publications 50, Oxford, UK:SLG Press, 1980.

These letters describe the life of one totally devoted to life in Christ and describes how God uses him for the world around him. Certainly an example of a Seventh Mansion Christian.

They Speak in Silences, (By a Carthusian), Kalamazoo, MI: Cistercian Publications, 1966.

This work is a translation of two small books published originally in French by the Benedictine nuns of St. Priscilla in Rome, first published in 1948. It is a foundational piece for understanding silence as part of prayer and the spiritual life.

Appendix B: A Mansions Comparison

The charts on the following pages are designed to give you a comparison of the Mansions at a glance. The goal is to give perspective on the kinds of things the God might be doing in you during a particular season of your journey.

	0	Mansion 1	2	3
	Outside the Castle	New Christian	Divided Loyalties	Discipleship: Life in Order
		First Water	*First Water*	*First Water*
Conditions of the Soul:	Dead in sin; self-focused; materialism	Initial faith; avoid offending God; focus on worldly cares	Saved, but ambivalent; half attachment to worldly pastimes.	Convinced God's way is right. Desire to live a life pleasing to God and useful to His Kingdom.
Actions by the Person:	Sinful behavior; little need of God	Attempts to rid oneself of sin; perform good works, religious activity.	Looks for God's leading through conversation, sermons, reading, trials all contribute to hearing God's call	Avoids even minor sins; awareness of sinful motives; good use of time; hours in recollection; gains greater knowledge of God through service
Nature of Prayer:	Deliverance and blessing	Requests for help/guidance, but scarcely see His Light	More receptive to divine promptings and grace; Divine light through prayer.	Mostly talking to God. Some discursive meditations on Scripture, nature; yet little joy, some peace.
Influence of God:	Calling of the Gospel; image and likeness influence	God responds to requests for help and through circumstances of life	Ceaselessly calling and responding to attempts to follow God's way	Guides in ministry, but few spiritual delights. Teaches through minor testings and experiences.

	0	Mansion 1	2	3
	Outside the Castle	New Christian	Divided Loyalties	Discipleship: Life in Order
Schemes of the Enemy:	Demonic deception, temptation	Puff them up with worldly honors, ambitions and temptations	Intensified attacks, through the deception of pleasures. Lie: "temptation is sin".	More subtle: Distractions from contact with God; Pride in attained levels of order and control.
Movements of Growth:	Exposure to the Gospel and desire for meaning and help from God.	Knowledge of Scripture; self-knowledge and humbling. Community and mentoring	Perseverance, community and support. Scriptures applied to daily life. Spiritual warfare.	Humility – this is not the peak. Mentors who can point them into deeper more responsive relationship with God.
Scriptural Support:	Rom 1:18-32 Eph 2:1-7	Rom 9:25-26 Eph 1:17-21	2Th 2:13-17 Eph 6:10-18	Eph 4:17-24 Rom 12:1-3

	Mansion 4	5	6	7
	Touched by Love	Call to Unity	Spiritual Betrothal	Mystical Union
	Second Water	*Third Water*	*Fourth Water*	*Fourth Water*
Conditions of the Soul:	Absorbed in knowing, seeking, loving God; transforming results of faithfulness to Gospel demands	Intensification; falling in love with Him alone, powering a life of devotion and service, yet there's the feeling that one can't serve God enough; grief over those not in his love.	Deep union; will fully occupied with God; no attachments to created things.	Relative lifestyle perfection; stability/serenity of the soul's center. Life in the transcendent present. The reality of total emptiness apart from God. Deep inner joy despite circumstances.
Actions by the Person:	Mary and Martha work together: balance & integration of active ministry and inner reflection. Selects ministry activity by calling even over gifting.	Inner energies/senses are in union with Trinity's indwelling; inner liberty; other-centeredness. Mary & Martha work together to not only love but experience God.	Advances in God-centeredness: living the specifics of the Gospel, all of life holds the presence and will of God; constant joy in simplicity, humility and obedience.	Mary and Martha joined together: a complete integration of worship and work, of adoration and service, of being and doing. Life of service, great contributions.
Nature of Prayer:	Beginnings of responsive, vs. self-controlling prayer, and of infused contemplation -- Prayer of Quiet	Focused on contemplation, reaching for full union; no distractions in times of absorption: 10-15 min.	Communion with God beyond language and the senses; life in love with God; Mystical experience	Trusting silence; full union, spiritual marriage: adoring attentiveness that engenders full devotion.

148

	Mansion 4	5	6	7
	Touched by Love	Call to Unity	Spiritual Betrothal	Mystical Union
Influence of God:	Gentle and increasing awareness of God's presence and promptings in prayer and in life's activities.	Will and imagination taken up in God; more love than understanding. Dark Night of the Senses begins, where God hides so the faith grows without satisfaction, painful.	Wounds of love. Reveals Himself in deep experiences of Union and mystery. Healing	Deep union and intimacy that heals, transfigures and beautifies, giving peace and security, yet often leading to great sacrifice.
Schemes of the Enemy:	Distractions against contemplation and silence, though now less frequent, because used of God. Discouragement with typical Church.	Discouragement: progress feels like regression; Ridicule of those who do not know this love. Distractions of other's need.	Complete Dark Night of the Senses yield to Dark Nights of the Spirit: accusations that sin is the cause. Misunderstood by others.	Temptations, accusations and lies in are automatically repulsed and resisted. The Dark Night of the Spirit – God's presence not discerned is completed.
Movements of Growth:	Desire for solitude; habitual practice of prayer, vs. demand for productivity; deeper levels of warfare; mentor – interpreters.	Love of neighbor: service and extended silence. Mentors and community.	Increased responsiveness in prayer; service led by God. Silence and solitude. Extended prayer & elders for discernment.	"Intellectual" vision of Trinity, beholding the fullness of God that empowers; obedience in love, communion in service. God and other focus.

Appendix C: A Lenten Study in Transformation

The *Mansions of the Heart Study Guide* may be also be used as an individual or group study for the season of Lent. We suggest that you use the same overall format of the Study Guide, but substitute the Scriptural Readings and Personal Reflection Questions. While most Lenten small groups are designed for seven weeks, you may vary the number of weeks to fit your own schedule. The following Chapter assignments focus on the growth in the Teresian Mansions themselves in a seven week course.

A Lenten Study in Transformation – Seven Weeks:

Week 1	Chapters 1-3 & the following Introduction
Week 2	Chapters 4-5
Week 3	Chapter 6
Week 4	Chapter 7
Week 5	Chapter 8
Week 6	Chapter 9
Week 7	Chapter 10-11

Introduction:

The season of Lent, the seven weeks prior to Easter, focuses on the passion of our Lord Jesus and our forgiveness and redemption made possible through His suffering and death on the cross. While many Lenten studies end with the passion narratives of Good Friday, our study will put that all in context of the power of the resurrection. Through Jesus' suffering and death, forgiveness of sin has been made available to each of us though faith in Jesus Christ as our Savior. Through His resurrection, we are offered a new life in Christ where death no longer rules us and we live a life of transformation as the Holy Spirit recreates us in the image of Christ.

As a result, this life of transformation by the Holy Spirit can be seen through:

- the process of ridding us of the power of sin that would otherwise rule us
- the process of growing in love for God and others, and
- the healing of our hearts to be able to know God according to our created design.

From the perspective of the Teresian Mansions, we can focus on this process from the following passion and resurrection perspective:

First Mansion: We are reborn, through faith in Christ, from bondage to sin into a relationship as sons and daughters of God, forgiven for our sins, and empowered by the Holy Spirit. Although delivered from the condemnation for sin, we are only beginning to understand how deeply we are diseased by it.

Second Mansion: We are confronted, through the indwelling Holy Spirit, by the true nature of our sin and begin to glimpse the deformity that separation from God has created in us. We struggle against the schemes of the devil to keep us locked in our sinful behavior and rebellion against God. We've come to understand how we are created to live within the Ten Commandments, but also how impossible it is to stay within their safe fences. Now when God calls out to us, as He did to Adam and Eve in the garden, "Where are you," we respond, "I am here! Help me!"

152

Third Mansion: As we are drawn deeper into relationship with God, Jesus calls us to follow Him in loving our neighbors and partnering with Him in bringing in His Kingdom. In this growing relationship of discipleship, we learn to hear His voice and cooperate with His leading. We are again confronted and grieved by our sinful human nature that tries to resist self-sacrifice and to control our own lives. The Holy Spirit teaches and empowers us to learn from Jesus as He followed the Father faithfully, proclaiming the Gospel even unto His death on the cross.

Fourth Mansion: Having learned to follow Jesus faithfully, we now discover in greater degree the relationship of "son" which has been given us. Like Jesus, we focus on God and the new relationship of love that is offered to us. Captivated by His love for us, we long to know the Father as Jesus does, to discover what was lost through mankind's fall from grace.

Fifth Mansion: God's love so captivates us that we yearn to love Him fully and completely. We more fully see the sin within us which grieves us deeply. We long to become free to love God and others freely and fully. The Holy Spirit increases the healing and purging process within us to enable us to grow in our knowledge of God and to love others as Jesus does. Sin and attachments to this world are losing their grip.

The Dark Nights: Sin and death have been the atmosphere in which we have lived our whole lives. Now that we are truly tasting God's amazing light and love, God makes us aware of the utter depravity and darkness of sin. To the extent we can stand it, He gives us tastes of what it would be like to know God and yet be eternally separated from Him. We now understand more than ever before why the Son of God had to become the Son of Man and die for us.

Sixth Mansion: Now, loving God so much that we actually desire to share the sufferings of Christ, even to the point of death if needed, our focus moves from ourselves to our Lord and His focus on others. The Holy Spirit continues to transform our hearts so that we can commune more fully with God in love and follow Him intuitively. We see death to self as the doorway to resurrected life with Jesus in this world.

Seventh Mansion: In deep union with the Trinity, we share the sufferings and joys of our Lord as He calls out for the hearts of His lost sheep and shepherds those He has retrieved. While not yet enjoying the fullness of our final resurrection, we can participate in His resurrection power in ways that can no longer be hindered by sin.

These Lenten themes can be highlighted through study and reflection of the Teresian Mansions by substituting or adding the following Scripture passages in the section called Digging Deeper with the Biblical References, and substituting or adding Lenten Questions to the section called Reflection Questions.

Week 1:   Chapters 1-3   Intro to Spiritual Growth

Digging Deeper with the Biblical References
-   Genesis 2:4-24
-   Genesis 3:1-24

Reflection Questions.

1. During your growing up years, how would you have described sin?
2. In those years, what metaphor for God might you have used in relation to the subject of sin?
3. What sinful behaviors or "sins" have you found the most troubling and why do/did they trouble you?
4. Have you ever promised not to do something ever again and what success have you found?

Week 2: Chapters 4-5 First and Second Mansions

Digging Deeper with the Biblical References

- John 3:16-21
- Ephesians 2:8-9
- 1 Corinthians 1:4-9

Reflection Questions

1. To what degree did "deliverance from sin" play a part in your conversion?
2. Which have you found harder: receiving God's forgiveness or forgiving yourself?
3. Consider your history of temptation. Is the enemy using the same schemes against you that he did before? What are they?
4. To what extend have guilt and shame played a role in your history, and how do you deal with those dynamics today?

Week 3: Chapter 6 Third Mansion

Digging Deeper with the Biblical References

- Matthew 6:24-27
- Galatians 5:16-24

Reflection Questions

1. What makes it difficult for you to trust Jesus when He asks you to follow Him? When do you hear "men of little faith" in your heart? (Cf. Matt 6:30; 8:26; 14:31; 16:8; Luke 12:28)
2. What kinds of people are the most difficult for you to work with and why?
3. What is it about the rejection of others that bothers you?
4. What helps you recognize sin in your life and what do you do with it when you see it?

Week 4: Chapter 7 Fourth Mansion

Digging Deeper with the Biblical References

- Proverbs 8:17-21
- John 21:15-17 (Note: Jesus uses "agape" for love in his first two questions. Peter responds with phileo - "friend". In Jesus' third question, He uses the word phileo.) Insert the Greek meanings for love and sense the transition to which Jesus is inviting Peter.

Reflection Questions

1. What is it about Jesus that attracts you to Him? What frightens you?
2. Where are you in the transition of focus from: "I love Jesus because of what He did for me on the cross and because He is so good to me" to "I love Jesus no matter what He does for me."
3. In what way does your awareness of your sinfulness affect your intimacy with Jesus?
4. In what circumstances to you feel closest to Jesus? How intentional are you about entering those circumstances?

Week 5: Chapter 8 Fifth Mansion

Digging Deeper with the Biblical References

- Psalm 27
- 1 John 1:5 – 2:1-14

Reflection Questions

1. In your relationship with Jesus, as it relates to sin, with which of these comparisons that John uses do you most identify, and why?

   Children,
   Young men,
   Fathers.

2. How do you relate to the ancient "Jesus Prayer?" "Lord Jesus Christ, Son of God, have mercy on me, a sinner?"
3. When you are confronted with your sinfulness, which of the disciple's behavior do you tend to emulate: Peter who denied Jesus, Andrew who fled, or John who stayed by Jesus at His trial and at His crucifixion?
4. If you accompanied Jesus and his disciples into the Garden of Gethsemane on that last night, what would you do? Use your imagination to put yourself in the scene.

Week 6:   Chapter 9   Dark Nights

Digging Deeper with the Biblical References

- Psalm 63
- Matthew 27:41-46

Reflection Questions

1. Reflect on times when you felt that God had left you alone. What did you learn in retrospect?
2. Imagine the sins you most struggle with as demons with whom you are alone in the darkness, a darkness without the awareness of God's presence. What would you feel, want, do?
3. What helps you persevere in times when you feel alone and don't sense God's love and presence?
4. When does despair become a temptation for you?

Week 7:   Chapters 10-11 Sixth and Seventh Mansions

Digging Deeper with the Biblical References

- Isaiah 6:1-8
- Matthew 27:16-20

Reflection Questions

1. Where is "the mountain where Jesus told them to go" for you? Where and in what circumstance is it easiest for you to meet Jesus in the glory of His resurrection?
2. What makes it hard for you to live freely in the resurrection life Jesus has given you?
3. If Jesus were to appear to you physically, in his resurrected form, what would He do and say?
4. What does it mean for you to "pick up your cross and follow Me?" Can you do that in joy, or is that a struggle?

If the setting and the group is conducive, you might conclude this series with Holy Communion together.

ABOUT THE AUTHORS

Dr. Tom Ashbrook

Tom leads Church Resource Ministries' spiritual formation ministry, the Order *of Imago Christi*. *Imago Christi* develops spiritual formation resources and coaches Christian leaders and churches to be able to live and lead with a spiritual authority grounded in loving intimacy with Jesus. He provides spiritual direction and coaching for pastors and missionaries in various parts of the world and leads spiritual formation discovery seminars. Tom holds degrees in aeronautical engineering, management systems, pastoral ministry, and spiritual formation. Tom is author of *Mansions of the Heart: Exploring the Seven Stages of Spiritual Growth*, published by Jossey-Bass in 2009. He lives with his wife Charlotte in Pagosa Springs, Colorado. You can learn more about Tom's ministry at *Imago Christi*.

Dr. Ted Wueste

Ted lives in Phoenix with his wife and two children. After serving nine years as the Senior Pastor of a church he planted, he now serves as Executive Pastor of Spiritual Formation in a large evangelical church in Phoenix. In addition, Ted offers spiritual direction and spends time co-directing the *Spiritual Formation Society of Arizona* – a network and support to those involved in spiritual formation ministry. He holds an M.Div. from Western Seminary and an STM from Dallas Seminary as well as Doctor of Ministry in Leadership from Phoenix Seminary. Ted also serves as an adjunct professor in Spiritual Formation at Phoenix Seminary.

CRM EMPOWERING LEADERS

CRM (Church Resource Ministries: www.crmleaders.org) is a movement committed to developing leaders to strengthen and multiply the Church worldwide.

More than four hundred and fifty CRM missionaries live and minister in nations on every continent, coaching, mentoring, and apprenticing those called to lead the Christian movement in their settings. This results in the multiplication of godly leaders who have a passion for their work and who are empowered to multiply their lives and ministry. Through them, CRM stimulates movements of fresh, authentic churches, holistic in nature, so that the name of God is renowned among the nations. See www.crmleaders.org. Tom Ashbrook serves with CRM as the leader of *Imago Christi* (see below).

The Order of *Imago Christi* is CRM's spiritual formation ministry to Christian leaders around the world. *Imago Christi* is a covenant community that develops spiritual formation resources and coaches leaders and churches to be able to live and lead with a spiritual authority grounded in loving intimacy with Jesus. See www.ImagoChristi.org. Tom Ashbrook founded Imago Christi and plays an integral part in its leadership.

The desire of the *Spiritual Formation Society of Arizona* is to partner in fostering the spiritual formation movement in Arizona as we create an environment for discussing and experiencing the rich history of Christian spiritual formation and build together on that foundation. Through networking and co-laboring, our heart is to bring spiritual formation resources to Arizona and highlight what God is up to in our local area. www.sfsaz.org. Ted Wueste Co-Founded and Co-Directs the Society.

Desert Direction is a spiritual formation ministry in the Christian tradition, valuing the text of the *Bible*, centered on the *Trinity*, and emphasizing a *contemplative* approach. Spiritual formation is grounded in the ideas that we are always being formed by something and that God is always present in our lives. Therefore, learning to be attentive to His presence enables us to be formed by Him which is the greatest desires of our hearts. Desert Direction is a ministry designed to come along side people to help **awaken** desire, **adjust** perspectives, and live **attentively** in deepening intimacy with God as Father, Son, & Spirit. www.desertdirection.com. Ted Wueste blogs regularly on the Desert Direction site.

ORDERING INFORMATION

Mansions of the Heart Study Guide can be purchased online at mansionsoftheheart.com or at amazon.com. Bulk orders for groups or churches can also be purchased at mansionsofheart.com at a discounted rate.

NOTES

NOTES

32843635R00100

Made in the USA
San Bernardino, CA
17 April 2016